Flowers

Preschool/Kindergarten

Save time and energy planning thematic units with this comprehensive resource. We've searched the 1991–1998 issues of **The MAILBOX**® and **Teacher's Helper**® magazines to find the best ideas for you to use when teaching a thematic unit on flowers. Included in this book are favorite units from the magazines, single ideas to extend a unit, and a variety of reproducible activities. Pick and choose a bouquet of these activities to develop your own complete unit or to simply enhance your current lesson plans. You'll find everything you need in this book to teach with real flower power!

Editors:
Angie Kutzer
Allison E. Ward
Michele M. Dare

Artist:
Teresa Davidson
Kimberly Richard

Cover Artist:
Kimberly Richard

www.themailbox.com

©1999 by THE EDUCATION CENTER, INC.
All rights reserved.
ISBN# 1-56234-308-4

Manufactured in the United States
10 9 8 7 6 5 4 3 2 1

Table Of Contents

Thematic Units...

from The MAILBOX® magazine.

Bursting Into Bloom!

Your little sprouts are sure to blossom as you dig into this bouquet of flower-themed learning ideas.

ideas by dayle timmons

Down And Dirty

Get your flower unit started by getting down and getting dirty—really! To prepare to grow a garden of marigolds this spring and summer, first locate a plot that is away from active playground areas, close to an outdoor water source, and in a sunny area. Prior to asking your children to join you at the spot, outline the section and loosen the grass and soil if necessary. Request that parents dress their children for several consecutive days in clothes that can be soiled. During your outdoor times on those days, supervise children as they freely dig in the soil to prepare it for gardening. After several days of laying the ground-work (better known as playing in the dirt!), rake the soil to smooth the dirt and prepare for planting the seeds. This is the way we dig the dirt, dig the dirt, dig the dirt. This is the way we dig the dirt; we're learning about gardening!

Bordering On Beautiful

Now that the field of your dreams is ready, you need a cool kid-made border for your garden. Border the area with large rocks or prebuilt wooden fencing (available at home-supplies stores). Invite children to use various colors of acrylic paints to paint the rocks or fence. Not only does this project give each child more input into creating your garden; it also adds color before the flower festival even begins!

Planting The Seeds

To help your gardening project "suc-seed," ask parents to send varieties of marigold seeds to school. Carefully open the packages; then empty the seeds into labeled resealable plastic bags. Laminate the packages. Staple one package of each variety to a tongue depressor to prepare labels for your garden. Place the remaining packages in your writing center or in your math center for sorting practice. Then take the seeds, the labels, some gardening tools, and your gardeners out to the garden to plant some seeds.

Garden Snakes

No need to be afraid of these garden snakes! To keep birds and small critters away from your newly planted garden, have youngsters paint these colorful reptiles. Provide pictures of real snakes. If possible, have each child find his own stick to paint using acrylic paints. Or give each of several groups of children a stick to paint. When the paint is dry, alternate putting each different snake in the garden. Ssss, gotcha!

A Blooming Surprise

Use this song to reassure youngsters that with some "TLC," water, and sunlight, their flowers will one day bloom.

Will My Flowers Bloom?
(sung to the tune of "The Wheels On The Bus")

The seeds from the pack go in the ground,
In the ground, in the ground.
The seeds from the pack go in the ground.
Will our flowers bloom?

Pretend to plant.

Palms up, questioning.

The rain from the sky goes drip, drop, drip.
Drip, drop, drip; drip, drop, drip.
The rain from the sky goes drip, drop, drip.
Will our flowers bloom?

Wiggle fingers downward.

Palms up, questioning.

The sun above is bright and hot,
Bright and hot, bright and hot.
The sun above is bright and hot.
Will our flowers bloom?

Form circle with arms overhead.

Palms up, questioning.

Our little seeds are sprouting fast,
Sprouting fast, sprouting fast.
Our little seeds are sprouting fast.
Look! Our flowers bloomed!

Slowly wiggle fingers upward.

Palms open beside face.

MARIGOLD

50¢

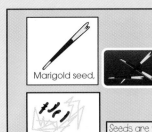

Marigold seed,

Seeds are tiny.

marigold sprout,

Seeds sprout.

marigold buds,

marigold flowers,

marigold seeds!

Watch What Develops

So what are we waiting for? Make a marigold timeline to help youngsters know what to watch for throughout the gardening project. Also use the display to document the garden's growth with real photos and youngsters' thoughts and illustrations. To prepare the timeline, duplicate a copy of the booklet pages (page 11). Color and cut out the pages; then glue them sequentially onto a length of bulletin-board paper. Refer to the illustrations as you discuss the stages. Take pictures of your garden in each of the corresponding stages. Display the real photos on the display along with youngsters' comments and artwork. After your project, laminate the photos; then place them in a science center to encourage discussions and sequencing practice.

Pretty Maids (And Masters) In A Row

In addition to your outdoor garden—or in place of it if outdoor space is limited—plant these windowsill gardens. Provide each child with a small, recycled container such as a yogurt cup or milk carton. Direct each child to fill the container with soil; then plant several marigold seeds. Provide a magnifying glass for close observations and a water bottle for misting the sprouts.

Identify each child's planter with these floral labels. Prepare a tracer from the smallest pattern on page 10. Direct each child to trace the pattern onto yellow or orange construction paper, then cut it out. Personalize each child's flower; then attach his picture to it. Next have each child paint a tongue depressor green. When the paint is dry, glue his flower to the depressor; then insert it into his planter. At the end of your gardening project, send these flowers home to be shared with families.

Marigold Merriment

Flowers won't be the only things emerging when you use this booklet idea to develop your little ones' prereading skills. Using the largest flower pattern on page 10, cut a flower shape from orange or yellow tagboard for each child. Duplicate a class supply of the booklet pages on page 11. Have each child color a set of booklet pages; then cut them out. Have him assist you in sequencing the pages; then staple them to the center of a flower shape. Merry reading!

Kara

Isaac

Marigold Merriment!

"Scent-sational" Flowers

While your little ones are waiting for their gardens to bloom, fill their time with a bouquet of flower-themed learning ideas. For starters, mix up several batches of flower-scented play dough. Store each scent of dough in a separate container labeled with flower pictures cut from a seed catalog. Place the doughs in a center along with flower-shaped cookie cutters, small plastic flowerpots, and painted green craft sticks for use as stems.

Scented Play Dough

3 cups flour
3/4 cup salt
3 tablespoons cream of tartar
1/8 cup powdered tempera paint (any color)
2 cups water
3 tablespoons oil
approximately 10 drops of potpourri oil (any floral scent, such as rose, gardenia, lavender, or jasmine)

In a large pot, mix together all of the dry ingredients. Stir in the water and oils until the mixture is smooth. Stir the ingredients over medium heat until the mixture forms into a ball. While the dough is warm, knead it on a floured board until it is silky smooth. When the mixture has cooled, store it in an airtight container.

Stop And Smell The Flowers

Let your school and parents know about your flower studies with this display that smells as good as it looks. To make a flower, use the middle-sized flower pattern (page 10) to cut a flower shape from a small, white paper plate. Use watercolors to paint the shape. When the paint is dry, glue a cupcake liner to the center of the plate. Add a few drops of floral-scented potpourri oil to a pastel-colored cotton ball. Glue the cotton ball to the center of the liner. Tape a length of green curling ribbon to the back of each child's flower. Attach the flowers to a wall or display so that they resemble a bouquet. Tie the ribbons together with a ribbon bow. Add the invitation "Stop And Smell The Flowers!"

Delicious Dirt

Now that your little ones have admired and smelled flowers, invite them to taste them, too! In advance, fill one ice-cream cone for each child three-fourths full of chocolate cake batter (prepared from a mix). Stand the cones in cupcake baking pans; then bake them according to the package cupcake-baking directions. Also cut off the pointed end of a supply of wooden skewers. To make one flowerpot snack, frost one of the cakes with chocolate frosting. Crush one chocolate-sandwich cookie in a bag; then sprinkle the crumbs over the frosting. To make each flower, put one gumdrop, a butter cookie, and then another gumdrop onto a skewer. Insert the flowers into the pot. Dig in!

A Rainbow Of Color

Isn't it amazing that flowers come in all the colors of the rainbow? With your class, look through a seed catalog or a reference book with photos of flowers. Encourage volunteers to identify the flowers by their colors. Then share the festive book *Planting A Rainbow* by Lois Ehlert (Harcourt Brace & Company). Use this crafty idea to find out which colors of flowers are your children's favorites. From shades of red, orange, yellow, blue, and purple construction paper, cut a quantity of the three sizes of flower patterns on page 10. Ask each child to find three different sizes of one color of flower shapes. Help him sequence the shapes, and then glue the centers together. Provide scraps of various colors of paper so that students can embellish their flowers, if desired. As a class sort the flowers by color; then arrange them on a green background for a display that's blooming with color.

Picking Flowers

Continue to cultivate color-recognition skills with this circle-time game. Using the smallest pattern on page 10, cut a class supply of flower shapes from various colors of construction paper. To play, seat the group in a circle; then ask a volunteer to stand inside the circle. Give each seated child a flower. Lead the group in the following chant as the volunteer moves around the circle. Direct the volunteer to pick a flower by the end of the chant. Then ask the child whose flower was picked to trade places with the first child. Continue until each child has picked a flower.

Pretty flowers grew out in the sun.
[Child's name] came to the garden;
She/He picked the [color] one.

Flower Child

Cultivate cutting skills with this crown of flowers. Use the smallest flower pattern (page 10) to prepare tracers. Invite each child to make a crown by tracing the desired number of flower shapes onto various colors of construction paper. Have him cut out the flowers, and then glue them onto a sentence strip. Staple the strip to fit the child's head. It's a crown of glory!

Youth Garden Grant

The National Gardening Association would like to help you cultivate young gardeners of the 21st century. If you have an outdoor school garden or plan to start one, request an application for the Youth Garden Grants Program. Three hundred schools and youth groups will be chosen for awards consisting of hundreds of dollars worth of tools, seeds, garden products, and educational materials. Consideration is given for innovative programming, sustainability, community support, strong leadership, and need. To receive an application, call 800-538-7476, extension 603; send a request to: Garden Grants, National Gardening Association, 180 Flynn Ave., Burlington, VT 05401; or E-mail the association at eddept@garden.org. Download an application from the web site at: http://www.garden.org. Deadline for completed applications is November 1.

Offshoots

Has your patch of marigolds got you hooked on gardening? For more ideas, request a complimentary issue of *Growing Ideas: A Journal Of Garden-Based Learning* (published by the National Gardening Association) by writing to National Gardening Association, 180 Flynn Avenue, Burlington, VT 05401. *Growing Ideas* provides instructional ideas, horticultural information, and a forum for exchange among teachers using plants to stimulate learning. Also check out the "Kids And Classrooms" section of the National Gardening Association's World Wide Web site: http://www.garden.org.

Digging Deeper

Flower Garden
Written by Eve Bunting
Illustrated by Kathryn Hewitt
Published by Harcourt Brace & Company

Alison's Zinnia
Written & Illustrated by Anita Lobel
Published by William Morrow & Company, Inc.

The Flower Alphabet Book
Written by Jerry Pallotta
Illustrated by Leslie Evans
Published by Charlesbridge Publishing

Counting Wildflowers
Written & Photographed by Bruce McMillan
Published by William Morrow & Company, Inc.

Flower Patterns

Use with "Pretty Maids (And Masters) In A Row" and "Marigold Merriment" on page 6. "Stop And Smell The Flowers" on page 7, and "A Rainbow Of Color," "Picking Flowers," and "Flower Child" on page 8.

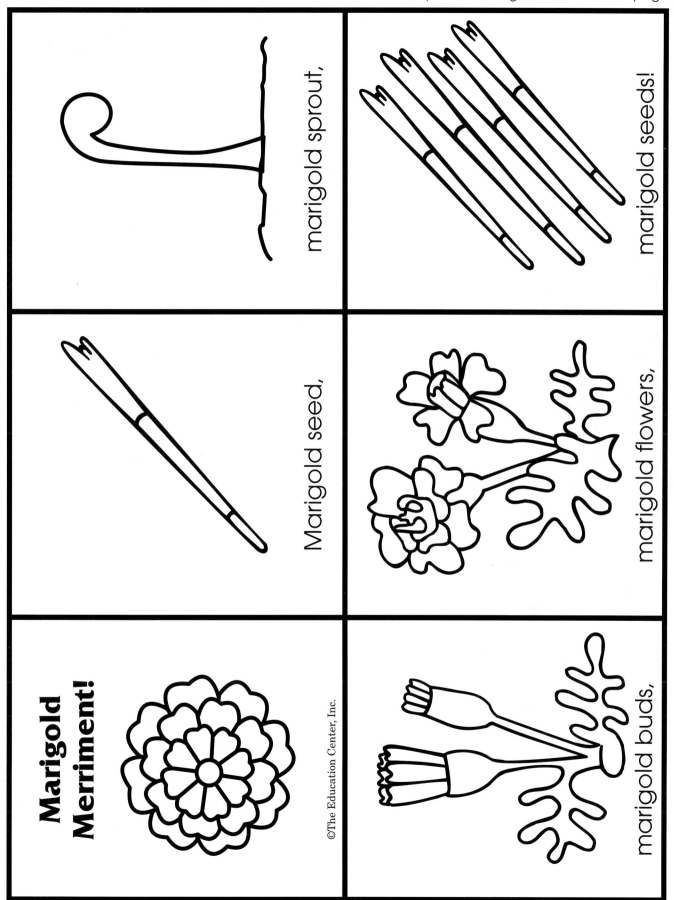

marigold sprout,

marigold seeds!

Marigold seed,

marigold flowers,

Marigold Merriment!

©The Education Center, Inc.

marigold buds,

Dandy Dandelions

Here's a dandy unit about everyone's favorite weed—the dandelion. Whether you're of the opinion that this bright yellow flower is a pest or a posy, you'll find the art, science, movement, and cooking activities to be delightfully fun. And we're not "lion"!

ideas contributed by Deborah Burleson

Dandy *Lion?*

Your little ones may wonder about the name of this bright yellow-and-orange flower. Some folks like to think that the dandelion looks like a lion's mane. The truth is, the word *dandelion* comes from the French *dent de lion* which means "lion's tooth." It was probably named this because of the dandelion's toothed leaves.

Take A Closer Look

Spring has sprung—and so have the dandelions! If you're going to be studying dandelions, you're going to need a bountiful supply of this wildflower. Take youngsters out for a dandelion hunt. Or request that parents help children look for dandelions in their own yards. Be sure to collect or request individual dandelion blossoms, blossoms that have lost their petals and turned to seed, as well as entire plants including the flower, stem, leaves, and root system. It may be helpful to know that dandelions blossom from May through June, and sometimes later, into the fall. And there's no need to worry about picking too many. Dandelions grow almost as quickly as the sun spreads its shine!

When you have a supply of the dainty dandelion, provide youngsters with hand magnifiers for taking a closer look. As a class, take the time to look at, smell, and feel the plants or flowers. You may discover that the blossom is actually made of more than 100 tiny flowers and that the stems are slightly hairy. Encourage careful observation with open questions such as, "How many fluffy seeds do you think this dandelion has?" or "Why do you think the leaves have jagged edges?"

Flower Or Fluff?

Is a dandelion still a dandelion when its flower turns to fluff? Absolutely! Use this crafty idea to discuss the stages and changes of a dandelion's growth cycle. Reproduce, color, and cut out the growth-cycle pattern on page 15. Sponge-paint a paper plate yellow. Paint a paper-towel tube green. When the paint is dry, attach the pattern to the center of the plate with a brad. Cut out construction-paper dandelion leaves; then glue them to the paper-towel tube. Tape the tube to the back of the paper plate.

Beginning with the picture of the seed in the ground, explain to youngsters how a dandelion seed grows, blossoms into a flower, turns into many seeds, and blows away to begin the process again. If desired, assist youngsters in making similar dandelions of their very own.

I'm A Dandelion

(sung to the tune of "I'm A Little Teapot")

I'm a dandelion,
Oh, so small.
I'm growing bigger;
Now I'm tall.

Soon my yellow blossom
Will turn to fluff.
Along will come the wind
With a great big huff.

Then my dandy seeds
Will dance around—
Traveling to places;
Floating to the ground.

*Crouch down.
Slowly rise.
Stand.*

Round arms over head.

*Turn in a circle.
Blow.*

Wiggle fingers above head.

Lower fingers to the ground.
—Deborah Burleson

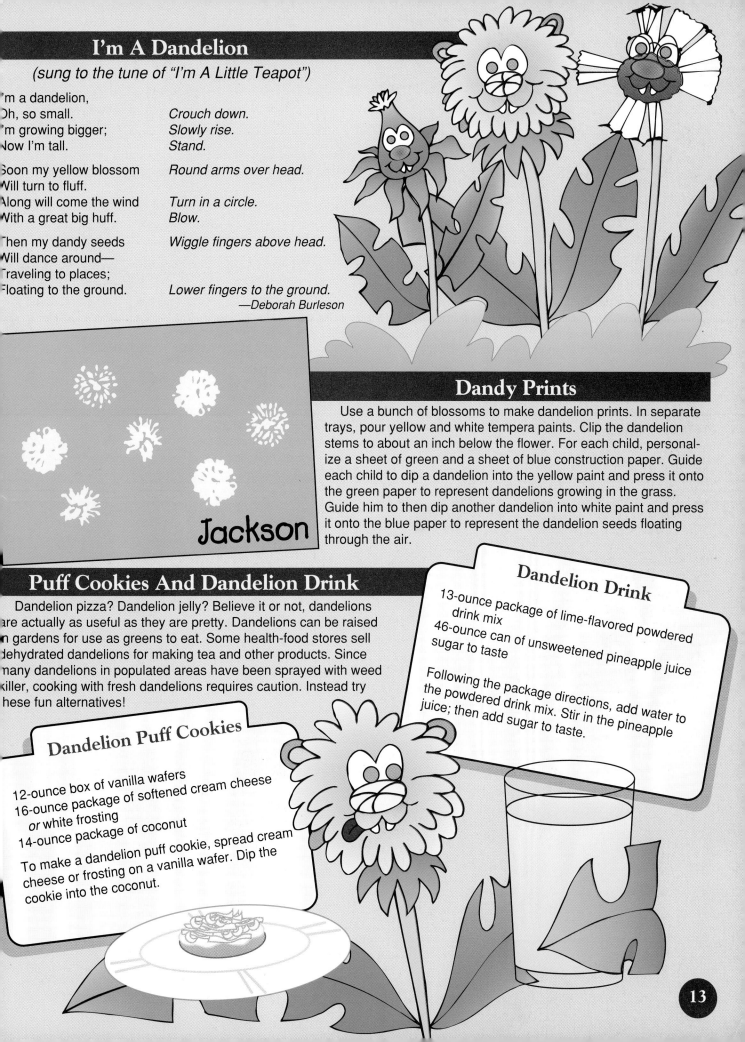

Jackson

Dandy Prints

Use a bunch of blossoms to make dandelion prints. In separate trays, pour yellow and white tempera paints. Clip the dandelion stems to about an inch below the flower. For each child, personalize a sheet of green and a sheet of blue construction paper. Guide each child to dip a dandelion into the yellow paint and press it onto the green paper to represent dandelions growing in the grass. Guide him to then dip another dandelion into white paint and press it onto the blue paper to represent the dandelion seeds floating through the air.

Puff Cookies And Dandelion Drink

Dandelion pizza? Dandelion jelly? Believe it or not, dandelions are actually as useful as they are pretty. Dandelions can be raised in gardens for use as greens to eat. Some health-food stores sell dehydrated dandelions for making tea and other products. Since many dandelions in populated areas have been sprayed with weed killer, cooking with fresh dandelions requires caution. Instead try these fun alternatives!

Dandelion Drink

13-ounce package of lime-flavored powdered drink mix
46-ounce can of unsweetened pineapple juice
sugar to taste

Following the package directions, add water to the powdered drink mix. Stir in the pineapple juice; then add sugar to taste.

Dandelion Puff Cookies

12-ounce box of vanilla wafers
16-ounce package of softened cream cheese
  or white frosting
14-ounce package of coconut

To make a dandelion puff cookie, spread cream cheese or frosting on a vanilla wafer. Dip the cookie into the coconut.

13

Giant Dandelions And Puffballs

Make these dandelions and puffballs to use with the outdoor and fingerplay ideas on this page, or as manipulatives during math activities. Cut a 4" square from cardboard. Wrap a length of yellow or white yarn (about 6 1/2 yards long) around the square 100 times. Carefully slide the wrapped yarn off the cardboard; then tie and knot a length of yarn around the center of the looped yarn. Cut the loops; then shape the ball. These fluffy flowers never fade!

Happy Dandelions

Using the directions in "Giant Dandelions And Puffballs," make ten dandelions and ten puffballs. Ask ten volunteers to stand in a line; then give each volunteer one dandelion and one puffball. Ask each child to hold the dandelion in front of him with one hand and the puffball behind his back with the other hand. As you recite each verse of this rhyme, ask one student to switch the position of the dandelion and puffball so that the dandelion is hidden behind his back and the puffball is in front of him.

Pam Crane

Ten happy dandelions
Growing in a line.
One turned to fluff and
Then there were nine.

Nine happy dandelions
Growing by the gate.
One turned to fluff and
Then there were eight.

Eight happy dandelions
Growing toward heaven.
One turned to fluff and
Then there were seven.

Seven happy dandelions
Growing to be picked.
One turned to fluff
And then there were six.

Six happy dandelions
Growing up with pride.
One turned to fluff and
Then there were five.

Five happy dandelions
Growing more and more.
One turned to fluff and
Then there were four.

Four happy dandelions
Growing wild and free.
One turned to fluff and
Then there were three.

Three happy dandelions
Growing just for you.
One turned to fluff and
Then there were two.

Two happy dandelions
Growing in the sun.
One turned to fluff and
Then there was one.

One happy dandelion
Having lots of fun.
It turned to fluff and
Then there were none!

—Deborah Burleson

Puffball Toss

Once you've made a supply of puffballs, go outside for a round of puffball toss. Encourage students to toss the puffballs to partners. Or challenge them to toss the puffballs into baskets. Encourage any student who wishes to play independently to close his eyes, toss the ball into the air, then open his eyes to discover where the ball landed.

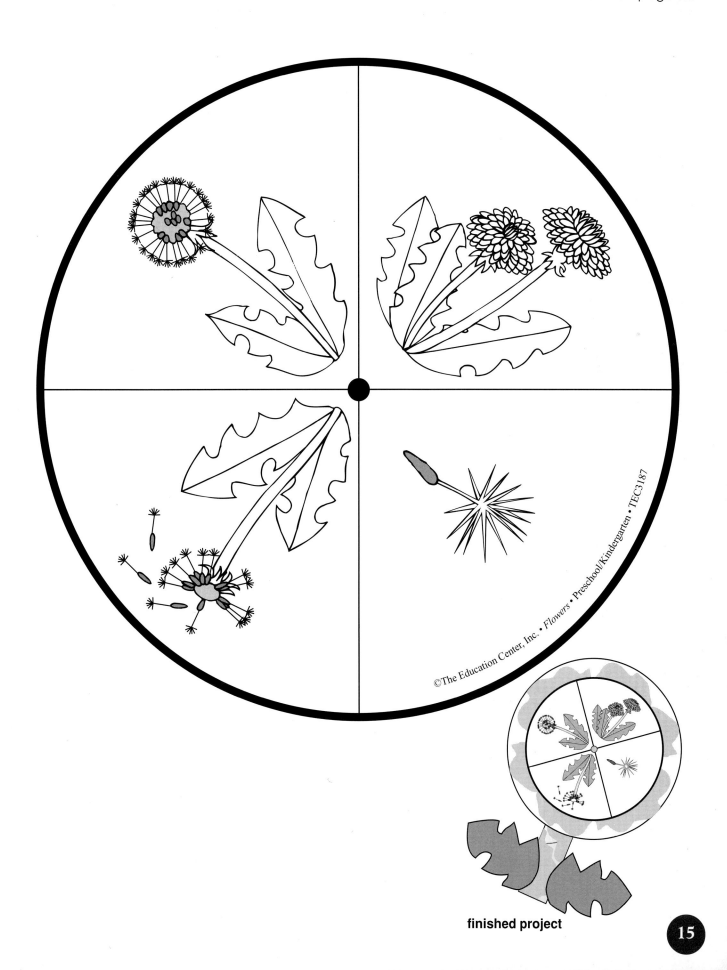

finished project

Flowers

Cultivate blooming minds with this bouquet of flower-themed learning activities.

by Lucia Kemp Henry

Paper-Plate Posies

Armed with a few posy-making suggestions, luncheon-size paper plates, and their natural creativity, youngsters will soon propagate enough perky blossoms to crowd any classroom bulletin board. In preparation for this activity, have students help you collect an assortment of construction-paper and gift-wrap scraps, tissue paper, geometrically shaped sponges, seeds, buttons, and cereal or pasta. Place the construction materials at different stations so that students who visit a station have the materials necessary to assemble one of three flower projects. For the first type of flower, have students crumple tissue paper into balls about the size of Ping-Pong balls. Then have them glue seeds to the center backs of paper plates and glue the tissue-paper balls around the plate rims. At another station, have students glue buttons to the center backs of paper plates, then glue one-inch wide gift-wrap strips to the plate rims. At a third station, have students repeatedly sponge-paint geometric shapes onto black construction paper. When the paint is dry, instruct students to cut around their shapes, leaving a margin of black around each design. To complete the project, each student glues cereal or pasta to the center back of a paper plate and glues his cutouts to the plate rim. Display these flowers on a bulletin board atop thick yarn stems embellished with construction-paper leaves.

Pots In The Sandbox

Use inexpensive plastic flowerpots in your sandbox or at your sandtable to generate lots of learning fun. Place a variety of sizes of pots, miniature trowels, and lima beans in your sand area. Encourage students to use the trowels to fill each of the pots with sand before "planting" the beans. Also ask students to arrange the pots from smallest to largest.

Potted Posies

Cultivate your youngsters' math skills at this bloom-filled center. Collect 11 inexpensive medium-size pots. Cut a Styrofoam® circle to fit the opening of each pot. Spray-paint the circles brown, if desired. Use a pencil to poke a different number of holes in each of the circles. Label each pot with a numeral to match the number of holes in one of the circular pieces. Insert each Styrofoam® circle in its matching pot. At the center with the pots, provide two pairs of children's gardening gloves, two gardening hats, and single-bloom plastic or silk flowers (one flower per pencil hole). To use the center, a pair of youngsters dons the hats and gloves and places flowers in the pots to match the numerals.

To convert this center to a color-word recognition center, replace the numeral labels with color-word labels and provide flowers in corresponding colors.

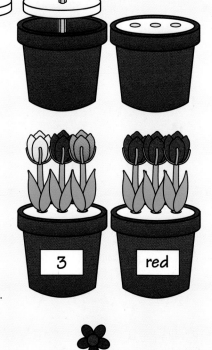

An Action Poem

Teach your youngsters this action poem that hints at the relationship between bees and flowers. Then, to provide more information about pollination, read aloud and discuss *The Reason For A Flower* by Ruth Heller (published by Grosset & Dunlap).

The Flower And The Bee

Here is a great big flower.	*Hold up open left hand with fingers spread.*
Here is a tiny bee.	*Press thumb and index finger of right hand together.*
The bee flies by with a buzz, buzz, buzz.	*Move right hand around to simulate flight of bee.*
The flower says, "Visit me!"	*Wave open left hand from side to side.*
The bee lands on the flower	*Set bee (right hand) on open palm of left hand.*
And does a dance so neat.	*Dance in place.*
He wiggles his wings and turns around	*Flap arms and turn around.*
And stomps his little bee feet.	*Stomp feet.*
The flower waves its petals	*Sway and wave arms.*
The bee hums a good-bye tune.	*Wave good-bye with right hand and hum.*
He flies away with a buzz, buzz, buzz.	*Move right hand around to show bee's flight.*
The flower says, "Come back soon!"	*Wave good-bye with open left hand.*

by Lucia Kemp Henry

Garden Flowers

Take a stroll in a lovely literary garden by reading *The Rose In My Garden* by Arnold and Anita Lobel (published by Greenwillow Books). This cumulative story uses rhymes and a surprise ending to keep young listeners entertained. Point out each new flower as it is introduced. To extend the theme of the book, teach your youngsters this simple song (sung to the tune of "Have You Ever Seen A Lassie?").

There's A Little Flower

There's a little flower.	A flower so neat!
A flower, a flower.	It's a rose so sweet.
There's a little flower	There's a little flower
On my garden path.	On my garden path.

Continue singing additional verses to the song, replacing the word *rose* in the second verse with *hollyhock*, *marigold*, *zinnia*, *daisy*, *bluebell*, *lily*, *peony*, *pansy*, *tulip*, and *sunflower*.

Fabulous Flower Centers

Use the flower and pot patterns (page 21) and the flower sequencing cards (page 27) to make several basic skills centers. To use the flower and pot designs (page 21), duplicate the patterns on white construction paper and color as desired. Program the upper and lower halves for the matching activity of your choice. Cut on the bold line to separate each flower from its pot.

To use the sequencing cards (page 27), duplicate the cards on white construction paper. Then color and cut them out. Students may sequence a single set of cards. Or, if multiple cards are used, have students find same-sized cards.

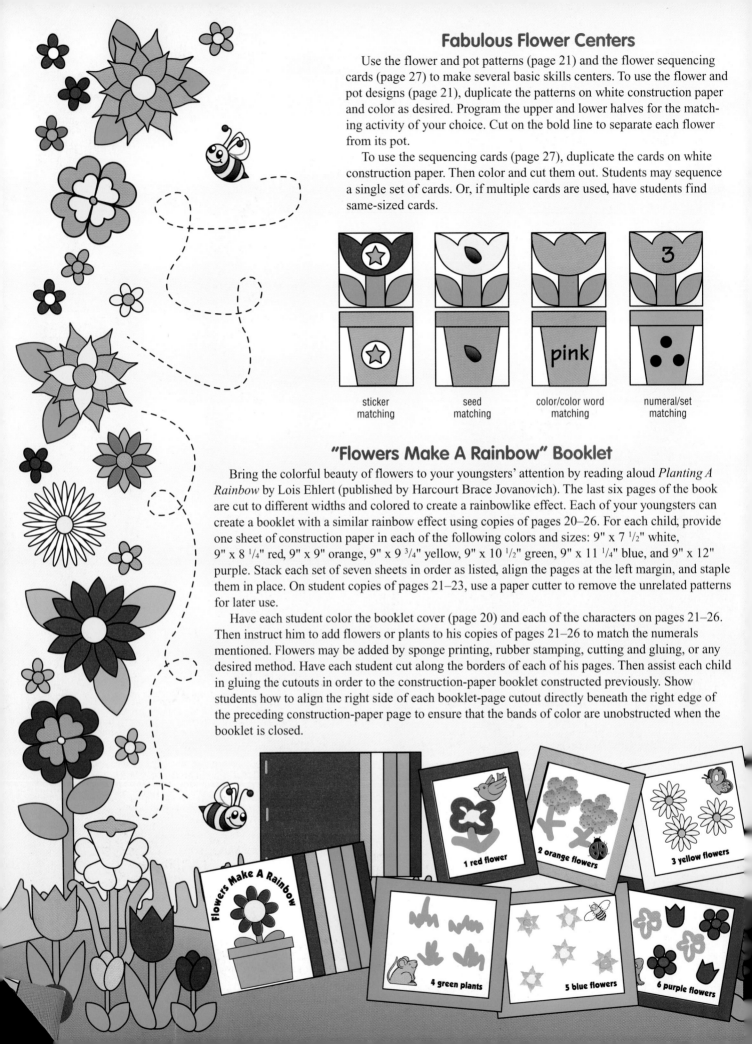

sticker matching

seed matching

color/color word matching

numeral/set matching

"Flowers Make A Rainbow" Booklet

Bring the colorful beauty of flowers to your youngsters' attention by reading aloud *Planting A Rainbow* by Lois Ehlert (published by Harcourt Brace Jovanovich). The last six pages of the book are cut to different widths and colored to create a rainbowlike effect. Each of your youngsters can create a booklet with a similar rainbow effect using copies of pages 20–26. For each child, provide one sheet of construction paper in each of the following colors and sizes: 9" x 7 1/2" white, 9" x 8 1/4" red, 9" x 9" orange, 9" x 9 3/4" yellow, 9" x 10 1/2" green, 9" x 11 1/4" blue, and 9" x 12" purple. Stack each set of seven sheets in order as listed, align the pages at the left margin, and staple them in place. On student copies of pages 21–23, use a paper cutter to remove the unrelated patterns for later use.

Have each student color the booklet cover (page 20) and each of the characters on pages 21–26. Then instruct him to add flowers or plants to his copies of pages 21–26 to match the numerals mentioned. Flowers may be added by sponge printing, rubber stamping, cutting and gluing, or any desired method. Have each student cut along the borders of each of his pages. Then assist each child in gluing the cutouts in order to the construction-paper booklet constructed previously. Show students how to align the right side of each booklet-page cutout directly beneath the right edge of the preceding construction-paper page to ensure that the bands of color are unobstructed when the booklet is closed.

Flowers Make A Rainbow

1 red flower

2 orange flowers

3 yellow flowers

4 green plants

5 blue flowers

6 purple flowers

Skit Props

Construct these simple props to add pizzazz and color to flower play. To make a large flower-shaped color-word card for each student in the play, use the fold-out flower pattern on page 28. Reproduce the pattern onto tagboard and cut it out along the solid lines. Fold a 12" x 18" sheet of colored construction paper in half. Place the flower pattern on the fold as indicated. Trace around the pattern; then cut out the resulting outline. Unfold the paper. Use the dotted line near the center of the flower pattern to make a white oval cutout. Glue the oval to the first cutout for the flower's center. Fold the sides of the flower as indicated on the pattern. Unfold the flower and label the center with the corresponding color word, positioning the letters so that they will be covered when the flower is folded.

When using these flowers with "Flowers Make A Rainbow Skit," have each child hold his folded flower during the first line of his verse. But when the color word is mentioned in the last line of the verse, instruct him to unfold the flower. During the last verse of the poem, have all students stand with their flower above their heads, creating a rainbow effect.

Mother's Day Floral Tea Party

Plan a tea party with a fresh floral theme to honor your students' moms, female relatives, and friends. Without cutting the flower and pot patterns apart, use the patterns on page 21 to make simple party invitations. Then adapt the fold-out flower pattern on page 28 so that students can make Mother's Day cards. For the guests, flowered headbands can be made using the patterns on page 22. During the tea party serve student-made flower-shaped sugar cookies along with tea or punch. If your students' rainbow books are still at school, ask each student to read his to his guest before she leaves.

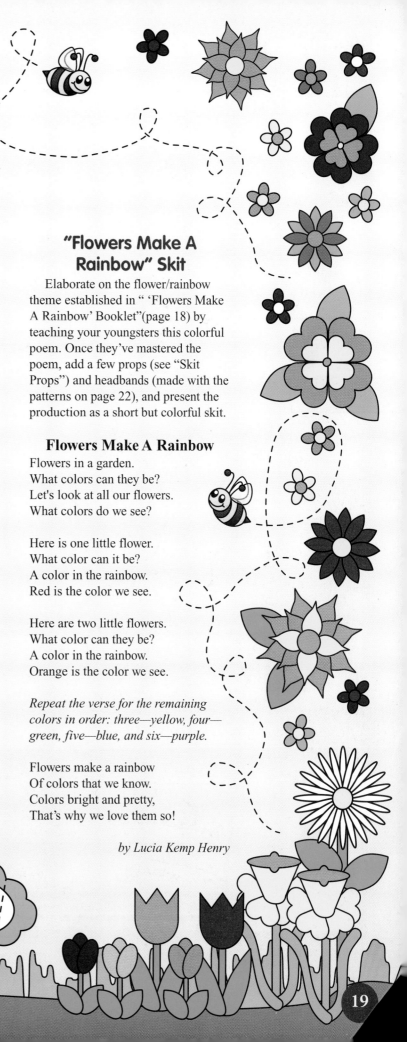

"Flowers Make A Rainbow" Skit

Elaborate on the flower/rainbow theme established in " 'Flowers Make A Rainbow' Booklet"(page 18) by teaching your youngsters this colorful poem. Once they've mastered the poem, add a few props (see "Skit Props") and headbands (made with the patterns on page 22), and present the production as a short but colorful skit.

Flowers Make A Rainbow

Flowers in a garden.
What colors can they be?
Let's look at all our flowers.
What colors do we see?

Here is one little flower.
What color can it be?
A color in the rainbow.
Red is the color we see.

Here are two little flowers.
What color can they be?
A color in the rainbow.
Orange is the color we see.

Repeat the verse for the remaining colors in order: three—yellow, four—green, five—blue, and six—purple.

Flowers make a rainbow
Of colors that we know.
Colors bright and pretty,
That's why we love them so!

by Lucia Kemp Henry

Booklet Cover
Use with " 'Flowers Make A Rainbow' Booklet" on page 18.

Flowers Make A Rainbow

by

_____
name

©The Education Center, Inc. • *Flowers* • Preschool/Kindergarten • TEC3187

Flower And Pot Patterns
Use with "Fabulous Flower Centers" on page 18 and "Mother's Day Floral Tea Party" on page 19.

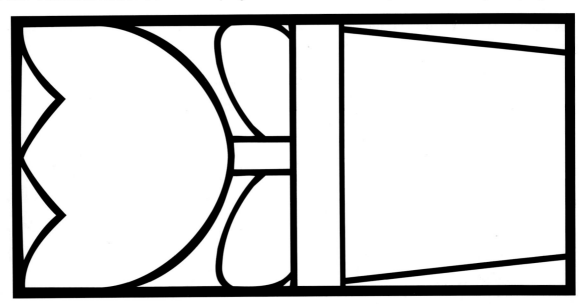

Booklet Page
Use with " 'Flowers Make A Rainbow' Booklet" on page 18.

1 red flower

Flower Patterns

Use with " 'Flowers Make A Rainbow' skit" and "Mother's Day Floral Tea Party" on page 19.

Booklet Page

Use with " 'Flowers Make A Rainbow' Booklet" on page 18.

2 orange flowers

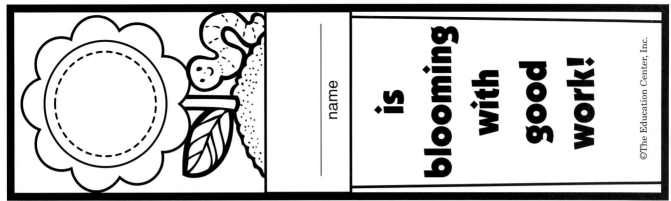

name

is blooming with good work!

©The Education Center, Inc.

Booklet Page
Use with " `Flowers Make A Rainbow' Booklet" on page 18.

3 yellow flowers

Booklet Page

Use with " 'Flowers Make A Rainbow' Booklet" on page 18.

4 green plants

5 blue flowers

6 purple flowers

Foldout-Flower Pattern
Use with "Skit Props" and "Mother's Day Floral Tea Party" on page 19.

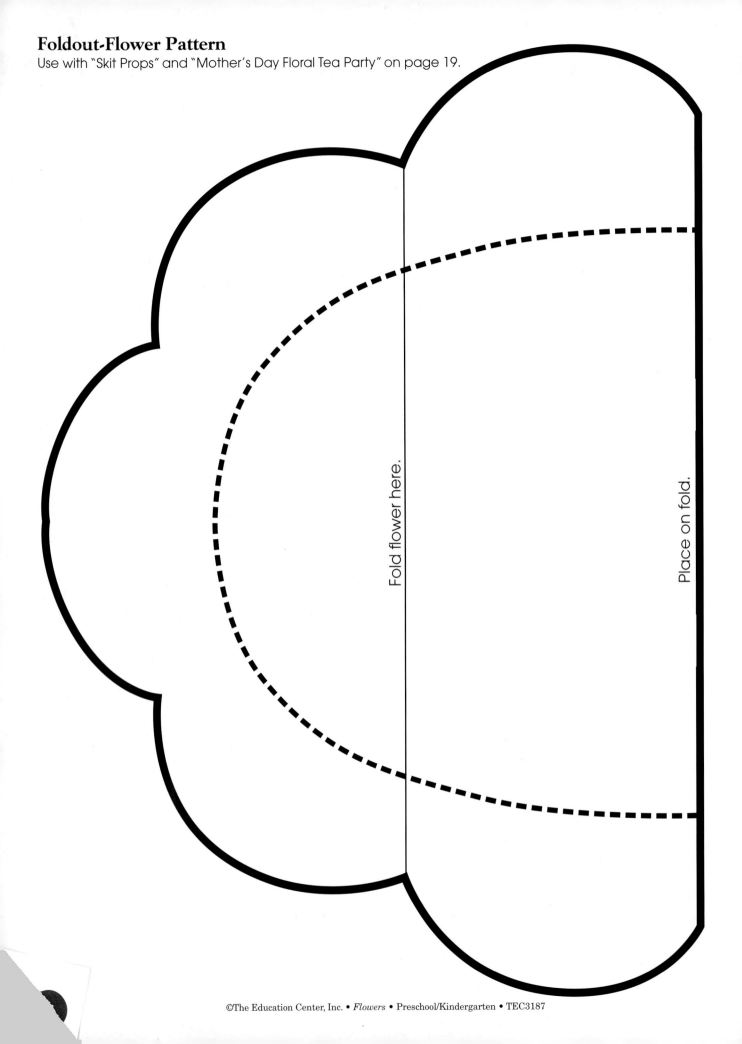

Fold flower here.

Place on fold.

Another Bouquet Of Ideas

Big Blossoms

Your youngsters can show off their green thumbs with these unusual flowers of original design. To begin, glue tinted pasta, rice, and glitter to a luncheon-size paper plate. When the glue has dried, mount the plate on tagboard along with a paper stem and leaves. Display these flowers on your classroom walls at baseboard level to create the effect of an oversize garden.

Linda Schwitzke
Headstart
Longview, WA

Finger-Frolicking Tulips

Excitement is sure to bloom when your little ones create these finger-painted tulips. Fingerpaint with a desired color onto fingerpainting paper. When the paint is dry, cut out a tulip shape. Next trace both hands onto green construction paper; then cut on the resulting outlines. To assemble the flower, glue the tulip to a green construction-paper stem; then glue the hand shapes to either side of the stem to resemble leaves. Personalize and write the date on the hand shapes. Cultivate these pretty posies on a bulletin board or window for a colorful display that's hands above the rest!

Lida Mills—Preschool
Hodgkins Park District
Hodgkins, IL

Blooming Bouquets

Your little ones will learn new art techniques with this creative project. To begin, tear a page from a book of wallpaper samples; then fold it in half either vertically or horizontally. Cutting away from the fold, cut out half of a vase shape free-hand. Open the paper and glue the vase cutout to a larger sheet of fingerpaint paper. Using a green marker, draw stems above the vase. Drop spoon-fuls of different colors of paint onto the paper on and above the stems. Lay a piece of waxed paper atop the paint; then press, pat, and roll the colors together. When the paint dries, remove the waxed paper. Trim the paper around the vase and bou-quet of flowers. Now that's creativity in bloom!

Bernadette Hoyer—Title I Pre-K, Brunner School
Scotch Plains, NJ

Pretty Posies

Cure spring fever with these perky window boxes brimming with posies. For window boxes, cover several shoeboxes with colorful gift wrap or Con-Tact® paper. To prepare for posy making, have students work together to paint a large supply of craft sticks green. Allow for drying time. Then have students make posies. To make a posy, select a flower pattern and trace it onto construction paper or draw a flower design freehand. Cut out the flower and glue it to a green stick along with a green paper leaf, if desired. Roll some modeling clay into a ball before flattening one side of the ball on a table-top. Insert the undecorated end of the stick into the clay, and place this self-standing flower in a window box. This spring fever prescription is a feast for the eyes!

Silkunas, Lansdale, PA

Garden On The Go

Invite each child to create his own fabulous flower-box garden. To make a flower box, have the child use paint pens to decorate the sides of an empty plastic hand-wipes container (with the lid removed). After the paint dries, have him fill his box with potting soil, then transplant a few flowering plants into the box. Encourage the child to take his flower box home to give to a special person.

Up Pop The Flowers!

Have your group form a circle—then get growing!

(sung to the tune of "Pop! Goes The Weasel")

We plant some seeds in the dirt.
The rain falls in a shower.

The sun comes out, and what do you know?
Up pop the flowers!

Pretend to plant seeds.
Raise arms; then wiggle fingers downward.
Children hold hands and squat.
Release hands. Pop up.

Joan Banker—Preschool
St. Mary's Child Development Center, Garner, NC

Daisy Biscuits

Excitement will surely be bloomin' when making delicious daisy biscuits. In preparation for this activity, you will need: a jar of jam or jelly, a can of refrigerated biscuits, kitchen scissors, and a cookie sheet. To make a daisy biscuit, cut five slits around the perimeter of the biscuit. With your thumb, make an indentation in the center of the biscuit. Fill the indentation with jam or jelly. Bake according to the directions on the biscuit can.

Maria Cuellar Munson—Gr. K, Garland, TX

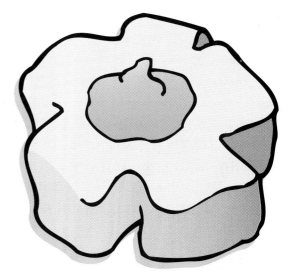

Flower Power Clock

If you're tired of checking time on a plain, round wall clock, then try this blooming good idea! From large sheets of yellow construction paper, cut a number of flower-petal shapes. Laminate the cutouts; then tape them on the wall around the clock so that it resembles a flower. The next time you check, time will flower and brighten your day.

Carol Denny—Three- And Four-Year-Olds
First Baptist Church, Conyers, GA

Flowers In A Row

A little gardening at this center will go a long way to keep letter recognition and/or phonics skills in bloom in your classroom. For each letter that you'd like to include, cut out a small construction-paper card. Label each card with a different letter; then glue a tongue depressor to the back of each card. Form vertical rows of sand; then "plant" the letter cards in your sand table, as shown. Next cut out a large supply of construction-paper flowers. Also cut out—or have your students cut out—letters/pictures from magazines. Glue each letter or picture to a flower; then glue a craft stick to the back of each flower. Place all of the flowers in a basket near your sand table. When a child visits this center, he takes a flower from the basket, then plants it in the corresponding row. He continues in the same manner until all of the flowers have been planted.

Kaye Sowell—Gr. K
Pelahatchie Elementary School
Pelahatchie, MS

Spring is in the air with this eye-catching display. Mount a large, paper flower—complete with title—on a wall. Have each child draw his face on a skin-toned, construction-paper circle. Have him glue his picture on a colorful piece of construction paper; then have him cut out a flower shape from the paper. Attach a long, paper stem to each flower. On leaf cutouts, write each child's dictation of things he enjoys doing in the spring; then attach the leaves to the stems. Mount the flowers on the wall.

Betty Jean Kobes—Preschool, West Hancock Elementary School, Kanawha, IA

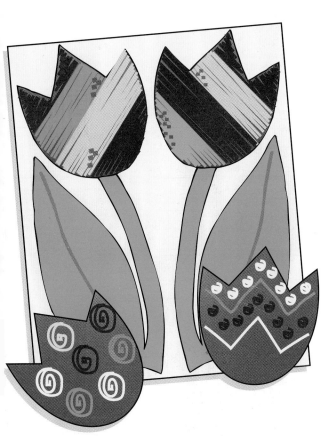

"Sand-sational" Flowers

Create a colorful "sand-sation" with this art idea that stimulates both the tactile and the visual senses. To make two tulips, trace tulip designs onto a strip of medium grade sandpaper. Use crayons to color each flower before cutting it out. Draw and color (or paint) stems and leaves on art paper. Glue the tulip blooms atop the stems. These flowers are so nifty your youngsters will be convinced they've sprouted green thumbs. So display the tulips on a bulletin board titled "Green Thumb Gallery."

Barbara Truex—Preschool
Union Methodist Nursery School
Federalsburg, MD

Tulip Planting

Initial consonant sounds blossom at this language center! Program each of a set of construction-paper pot cutouts with a different consonant letter. Then program tulip cutouts with pictures of things that begin with the programmed consonant letters. Attach a green construction-paper stem to each tulip cutout; then program the backs of the cutouts for self-checking. Laminate all cutouts for durability. Use an X-acto knife to cut a slit in each pot cutout; then store the cutouts in a flower pot. A youngster spreads the cutouts face up on a tabletop, then "plants" each tulip on the matching pot. When his planting is complete, the youngster "picks" each tulip and flips it to check.

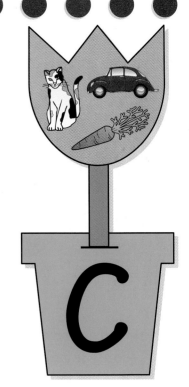

Barbara Paslet—Gr. K and 1 Special Education
Energy School, Benton, IL

Five Spring Flowers

Five spring flowers, all in a row.

The first one said, "We need rain to grow!"

The second one said, "Oh my, we need water!"

The third one said, "Yes, it *is* getting hotter!"

The fourth one said, "I see clouds in the sky."

The fifth one said, "I wonder why?"

Then BOOM went the thunder
And ZAP went the lightning!
That springtime storm was really frightening!
But the flowers weren't worried—no, no, no, no!
The rain helped them to grow, grow, GROW!

Flower Power

Counting, reading, number recognition, sequencing—they're all in this "kinder-garden." To create this center, make an enlarged copy of the flower, stem, and pot patterns below for each number that you'd like to include. Program each flower with a number word, each stem with a dot set, and each pot with a numeral. Color the patterns; then cut them out. To do this activity, a child sequences the pots, then matches each corresponding stem and flower. The result? A lovely display of learning.

Shelley Banzhaf—Gr. K
Maywood Public School
Maywood, NE

Tulips To Tiptoe Through

When you use this suggestion, your classroom will fill up with tulips so fast that there will be plenty to tiptoe through—if you're in the mood. To make a row of four tulips, accordion-fold a 12" x 9" sheet of green paper to 3" x 9". Trace the tulip plant pattern to the right onto the folded paper. Cut through all thicknesses, leaving the folds on the leaves and bottom of the plant intact. Unfold the paper. Trace the tulip bloom pattern below onto a piece of 3" x 7" paper that has been folded to 3" x 3 1/2". Cut on the resulting lines, leaving the folds on the top of the bloom intact. Repeat the previous two steps three more times for a total of four blooms. Keeping each tulip-bloom cutout folded, slip it over the front and back of a bloom area of the green cutout and glue it in place. These tulips look especially cheerful on windows or windowsills. Also consider taping several of these tulip rows together and stapling them to a bulletin board as a border so that the accordion-folds remain partially folded, creating a three-dimensional look.

adapted from an idea by Dorothy Burkley—Gr. K
Hartford Elementary School, Kinsman, OH

Tulip Plant Pattern

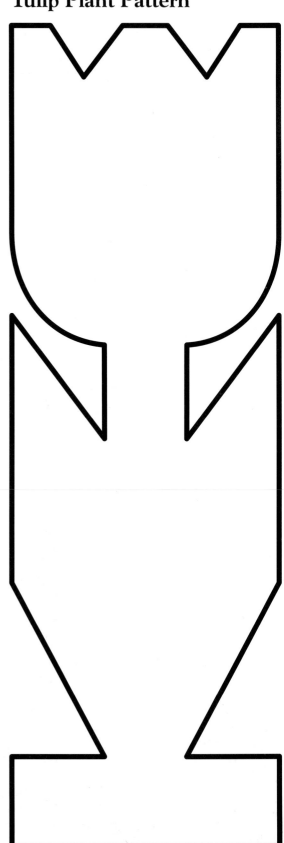

Place top of bloom pattern on fold.

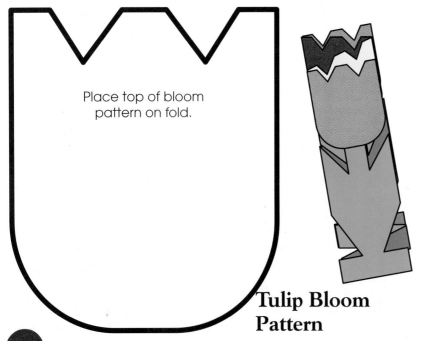

Tulip Bloom Pattern

Blooming Bingo

Sunshine is sure to fill your room during this blooming bingo game. To prepare, cut six flower petals and six squares from each of six different colors of construction paper. Also cut six strips of green paper to represent stems. Store each set of same-colored petals in a separate resealable plastic bag and store all of the squares in a paper bag.

To play this game with six children, give a stem to each child in the group. Ask each child to choose a set of same-colored petals to use as markers. Pick a square from the bag. Have the children name its color. Instruct the child who has the corresponding color of petals to place one petal on her stem. Each time a child completes a flower—by placing all six petals on her stem—she announces, "Blooming Bingo!" Continue picking squares until each child has completed her flower. Everyone's a winner!

Sheri McGarvey—Pre-K, Garrett's Way, Newtown Square, PA

In this case the more you add, the better it gets! Glue each child's photo inside a muffin liner. Mount the muffin-liner blooms along with construction-paper stems, leaves, and grass. Then encourage children to visit your art center and make spring things—such as butterflies, ladybugs, birds, rainbows, and clouds—to add to the board. How adorable!

Martha Ann Davis—Gr. K, Springfield Elementary, Greenwood, SC

Posies With Pizzazz

You can't beat the pizzazz these giant posies are going to bring to your classroom or to the hallway outside your classroom. To make one of these flowers, press both bare feet into a shallow pan containing a mixture of green tempera paint and dish soap. On a sheet of butcher paper, press your paint-covered feet to make the flower stem and leaves. Then press your hands into a shallow pan of red tempera paint and dish soap. Above the stem, make handprints for the flower's petals. In the middle of the handprints, glue a picture of yourself that has been cut into a circle.

Kaye Sowell—Gr. K, Pelahatchie Elementary School, Pelahatchie, MS

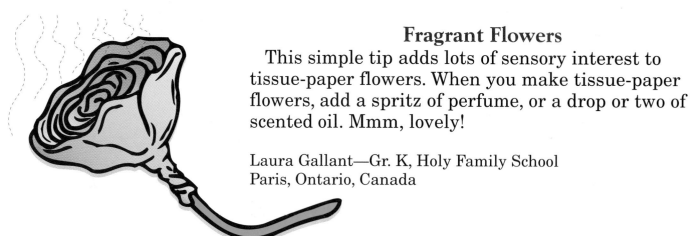

Fragrant Flowers

This simple tip adds lots of sensory interest to tissue-paper flowers. When you make tissue-paper flowers, add a spritz of perfume, or a drop or two of scented oil. Mmm, lovely!

Laura Gallant—Gr. K, Holy Family School
Paris, Ontario, Canada

Sleeping Beauties

Not all beautiful flowers grow from seeds that are planted in the spring of the year. Planting bulbs with children in the fall will produce a surprise crop of joy in the spring. To plant bulbs, you will need a patch of ground with good drainage. Show children the bulbs and explain to them that sleeping inside each bulb is a flower waiting for spring. Share with them that the bulb will need a snug space in a flower bed and a long winter's nap. Follow the directions included with the package for planting the bulbs. In the spring watch for tips of green to push their way through the ground. Wake up! It's spring!

Reproducible
Activities...

from TEACHER'S HELPER® magazine.

From Showers To Flowers...

Programming Suggestions For Page 41

— Program each of the flowers with the name of a learning center or an activity in your classroom. Have each child color the appropriate flower when she has completed each center or activity.

— Program each flower with a color word. Have each child color each flower the appropriate color.

— Program each flower with a simple addition fact. Have each child write the answer in each flower.

— Have each child color pairs of matching flowers the same color.

— Program each pair of flowers with rhyming words. Have each child color the rhyming flowers the same color.

Finished Sample

Name Charody   Open

From Showers To Flowers

red   orange   white

yellow   pink   purple

blue   green

From Showers To Flowers

Flower Power

How To Use Pages 42 And 43

1. Duplicate both pages on white construction paper for each child.
2. Have each child color and cut out the Tick-Tock Tulip and clock hands on page 43. Then have him lightly color and cut out the time booklet pages on this page. Stack the booklet pages, placing the booklet cover on top; then staple the pages.
3. Using a brad, assist each student as he pokes a hole at the dot on the clock.
4. Have each student use the brad to attach the clock hands to the clock cutout.
5. To use the tulip clock for telling-time practice, have each child turn to a page in his booklet, read the time, and move the hands on the clock to show the correct time.

Time Booklet

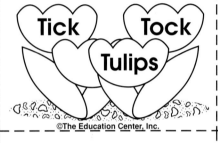

Tick Tock Tulips

©The Education Center, Inc.

1 o'clock   7 o'clock   4 o'clock

8 o'clock   11 o'clock   3 o'clock

6 o'clock   2 o'clock   10 o'clock

9 o'clock   12 o'clock   5 o'clock

Tick-Tock Tulip

Color. Cut. Assemble.

©The Education Center, Inc. • *Flowers* • Preschool/Kindergarten • TEC3187

Name _____

Tulip Time

Draw clock hands to show the correct time.

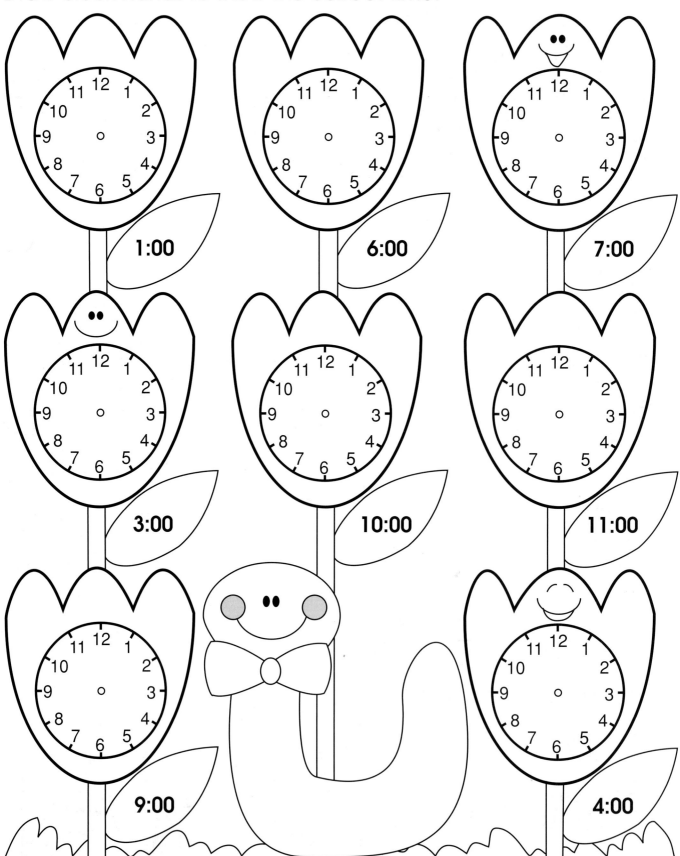

1:00

6:00

7:00

3:00

10:00

11:00

9:00

4:00

Name _____

Flowers By The Hour

Cut. Glue.

12:00	8:00

2:00	4:00	9:00	5:00

A Timely Tulip

 Cut and glue the numbers on the clock.

Fill in the blank.

It is _____ o'clock.

6   9   3   12   8   5

Watch Me Grow!

How To Use The Fold-Up Flower Award

1. Duplicate a copy of the award for each student.
2. Personalize each award. On the middle line, write a subject area or other area of achievement. Sign and date the award.
3. Have each student fold back on the bottom dotted line first.
4. Bring the fold up as shown to touch the upper dotted line, pressing down to crease the message portion behind the folds. Provide assistance as needed.
5. Encourage each child to color his award; then send it home with him.

Finished Sample

Watch Me Grow!

Name

is really blooming in

Teacher/Date

Flower Card

How To Make The Flower Card

 Cut out the card.

Draw a flower.

Color.

Fold the card accordion-style on the dotted lines.

Dear

My love for you grows,

and grows,

and grows,

and grows.

Love,